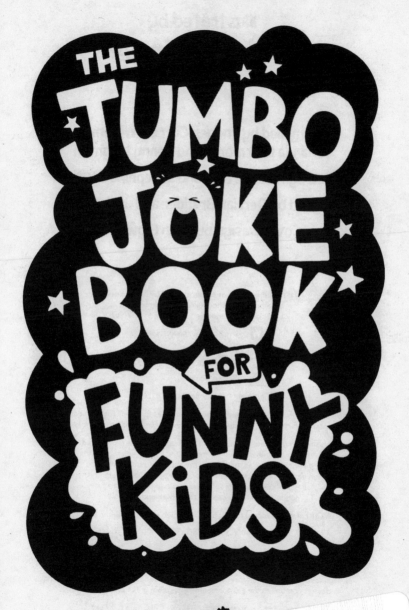

THE JUMBO JOKE BOOK FOR FUNNY KIDS

Buster Book

D0316702

Illustrated by
# Andrew Pinder

**Compiled by Imogen Currell-Williams,
Amanda Learmonth and Jonny Leighton**

**Edited by Helen Brown and Josephine Southon**

**Designed by Derrian Bradder and Jack Clucas**

**Cover Design by John Bigwood**

First published in Great Britain in 2020 by Buster Books,
an imprint of Michael O'Mara Books Limited,
9 Lion Yard, Tremadoc Road, London SW4 7NQ

W   www.mombooks.com/buster
f   Buster Books
🐦  @BusterBooks
📷  @Buster_Books

The material in this book previously appeared in *Jokes for Funny Kids: 6-year-olds*,
*Jokes for Funny Kids: 7-year-olds* and *Jokes for Funny Kids: 8-year-olds*.

A CIP catalogue record for this book is available from the British Library.

ISBN: 978-1-78055-716-8

2 4 6 8 10 9 7 5 3

Papers used by Buster Books are natural, recyclable products made of wood from
well-managed, FSC®-certified forests and other controlled sources. The manufacturing
processes conform to the environmental regulations of the country of origin.

Printed and bound in February 2021 by CPI Group (UK) Ltd,
108 Beddington Lane, Croydon, CR0 4YY, United Kingdom

MIX
Paper from
responsible sources
FSC® C020471
www.fsc.org

# CONTENTS

# Introduction

## Why don't monsters eat clowns?

Because they taste funny.

Welcome to this te he he-larious bumper collection of the best jokes for kids.

In this book you will find over 500 side-splitting jokes which will have you cracking up with laughter – from amusing animals and silly monsters to hilarious history and troublesome tongue twisters.

If these jokes don't tickle your funny bone then nothing will. Don't forget to share your funniest jokes with your friends and family and practise your comic timing!

Spooky and Kooky

**What do ghosts have for lunch?**

I-scream on toast.

**What do you give a ghost with bad eyesight?**

Spook-tacles.

**Which hockey position do ghosts like to play in?**

Ghoul-keeper.

**What do you call a crime-fighting ghost?**

A police in-spectre.

**What do ghost pandas eat?**

Bam-BOO!

**What are ghosts most afraid of?**

Public spooking.

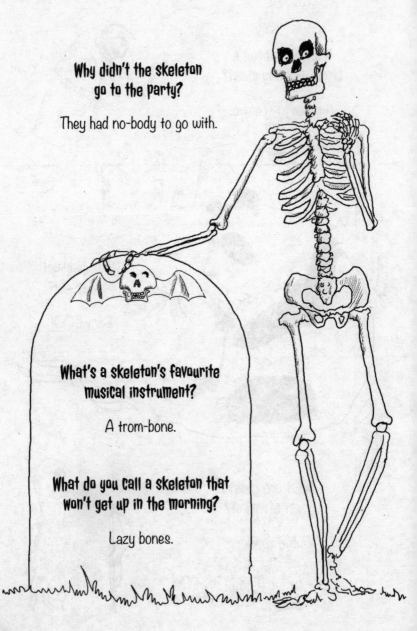

**Why didn't the skeleton go to the party?**

They had no-body to go with.

**What's a skeleton's favourite musical instrument?**

A trom-bone.

**What do you call a skeleton that won't get up in the morning?**

Lazy bones.

**What does a skeleton order at a restaurant?**

Spare ribs.

**How did the skeleton know it was going to snow?**

He could feel it in his bones.

**What do you call a skeleton who goes out in the snow?**

A numb-skull.

**What do you call a witch on a beach holiday?**

A sand witch.

**What's the problem with twin witches?**

You never know which witch is which.

**What do witches race on?**

VROOM-sticks.

**What's a witch's favourite school subject?**

Spelling.

**What kind of tests do witches do at school?**

Hex-ams.

**What do you call two witches who live together?**

B-room mates.

**What's a zombie's favourite type of weather?**

Cloudy with a chance of brain.

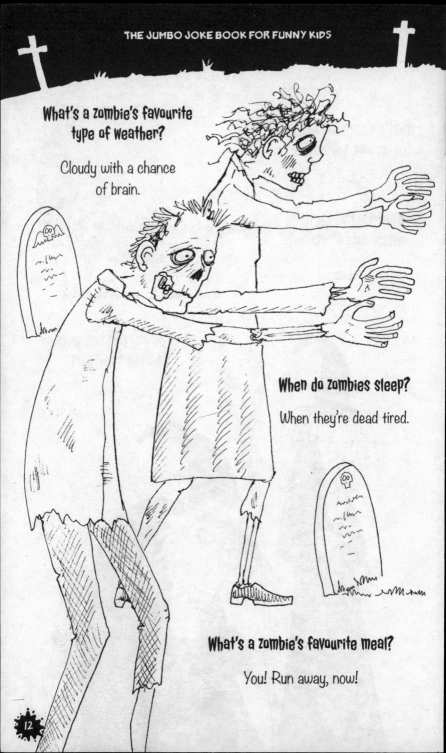

**When do zombies sleep?**

When they're dead tired.

**What's a zombie's favourite meal?**

You! Run away, now!

**How do you say goodbye to a vampire?**

See ya later, sucker!

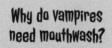

**What's a vampire's favourite type of dog?**

A bloodhound.

**Why do vampires need mouthwash?**

They've got bat breath.

13

**Why did the monster eat the tightrope performer?**

He wanted a balanced diet.

**What time is it when a huge monster sits on your house?**

Time to get a new house.

**What do you call a werewolf with no legs?**

Anything you like, it can't catch you!

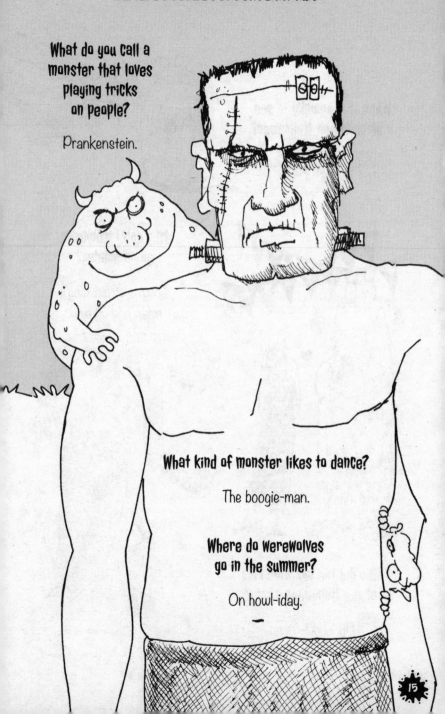

**What do you call a monster that loves playing tricks on people?**

Prankenstein.

**What kind of monster likes to dance?**

The boogie-man.

**Where do werewolves go in the summer?**

On howl-iday.

15

**When is it unlucky to see a black cat on Halloween?**

When you're a mouse.

**Why don't mummies go on holiday?**

They're afraid they'll relax and unwind.

**Who did the monster kiss at the Halloween party?**

His ghoul-friend.

**Why is it safe to tell a mummy your secrets?**

Because they'll always keep them under wraps.

**Ghoul:** Where do fleas go in the winter?

**Werewolf:** Search me!

**What do you do with a green monster?**

Wait until it's ripe.

**Which monster is the brightest?**

Franken-shine.

**What do you get if you cross a Scottish monster with a bad egg?**

The Loch Ness Pongster.

**How do you greet a three-headed monster?**

"Hello, hello, hello."

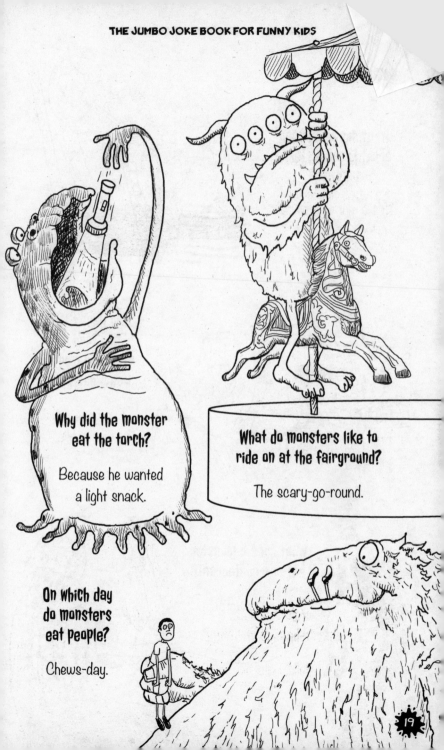

Why did the monster
eat the torch?

Because he wanted
a light snack.

What do monsters like to
ride on at the fairground?

The scary-go-round.

On which day
do monsters
eat people?

Chews-day.

19

### What did people say about Frankenstein's painting?

"It's a monster-piece."

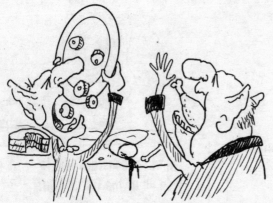

### Why wasn't there any food left after the monster Halloween party?

Everyone there was goblin.

### What does a monster eat in a restaurant?

The waiters!

**How do monsters like their eggs?**

Terror-fried.

**What's big, hairy, dangerous and has four wheels?**

A monster on a skateboard.

**How does a monster begin a story?**

"Once upon a slime ..."

**Why did the one-eyed monster give up teaching?**

He only had one pupil.

**What do monsters love to play at parties?**

Swallow the leader!

**What kind of cheese do monsters like?**

Monster-ella.

**How do monsters keep their fur looking neat and tidy?**

They use scare spray.

**Why is the letter 'v' like a monster?**

It comes after u.

**Knock Knock!**

Who's there?

**Butter.**

Butter, who?

**Butter run away, there's a monster behind you!**

23

**What kind of photos do elves like taking?**

Elfies.

**What do elves like to do in their spare time?**

Watch the tel-elf-vision.

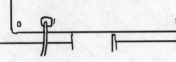

**Why did the monster knit herself three socks?**

Because she had three feet.

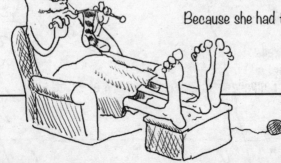

**Why do black cats prefer wizards to elves?**

Because they like sorcerers of milk.

**What do you call a wizard with fur?**

Hairy Potter.

**What happened to the naughty wizard at school?**

He was ex-spelled.

**What do you call a fairy that won't take a bath?**

Stinker-bell.

**Who granted the fish princess a wish?**

Her fairy cod-mother.

**What's the difference between a carrot and a unicorn?**

One's a bunny feast, the other's a funny beast.

**What did the dragon say when he saw the knight in shining armour?**

"I hate tinned food."

**What's big, scaly, breathes fire and bounces?**

A dragon on a trampoline.

**What's a dragon's favourite snack?**

Firecrackers.

What sound do you hear when dragons eat spicy food?

A fire alarm.

Why do dragons sleep during the day?

So they can fight knights.

Why are dragons good storytellers?

Because they have such long tails.

**Why is a dragon like a barbecue?**

They're always smoking.

**How do you compliment a dragon?**

Tell it it's claw-some.

**What do polite dragons say?**

"Fang you very much."

School Drools

**What kind of school do pilots go to?**

High school.

**What kind of school do surfers go to?**

Boarding school.

**Why do magicians make great teachers?**

They're always asking trick questions.

**What's the difference between a swamp and school gravy?**

Sadly, not a lot.

**How do elves learn to spell?**

They use the elf-abet.

**What object is the king of the classroom?**

The ruler.

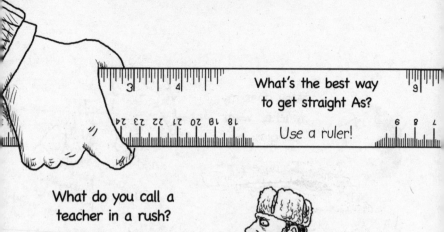

What's the best way to get straight As?

Use a ruler!

What do you call a teacher in a rush?

A Russian teacher.

Pupil: I didn't deserve zero out of ten on the last test.

Teacher: I agree, but it was the lowest mark I could give you.

Why does my
teacher wear
sunglasses?

Because I'm
so bright.

What do gnomes do
after school?

Gnome-work.

What's a snake's
favourite lesson?

Hissss-tory.

What do booklovers take fishing?

Bookworms.

Why did the music teacher carry a ladder around with him?

To reach the high notes.

Teacher: Why are you late?

Pupil: I'm not late, I'm EARLY for tomorrow!

# EXCUSES, EXCUSES ...

I didn't do my homework because ...

The dog ate it. (He said it was delicious.)

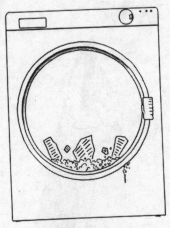

My dad put it in the washing machine. At least it's clean ...

I was abducted by aliens. And they didn't know the answers either.

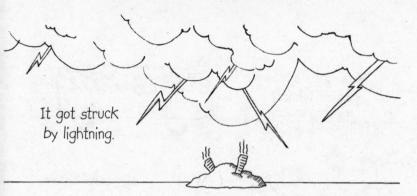

It got struck
by lightning.

A gust of wind
blew it out of
the window.

I'm allergic to
maths. It makes
me all itchy.

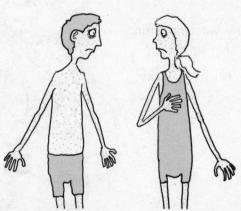

How does a bee
get to school?

It takes the buzz.

Why are fish so clever?

Because they're
always in schools.

Why was the Viking
ship so cheap?

It was on sail.

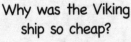

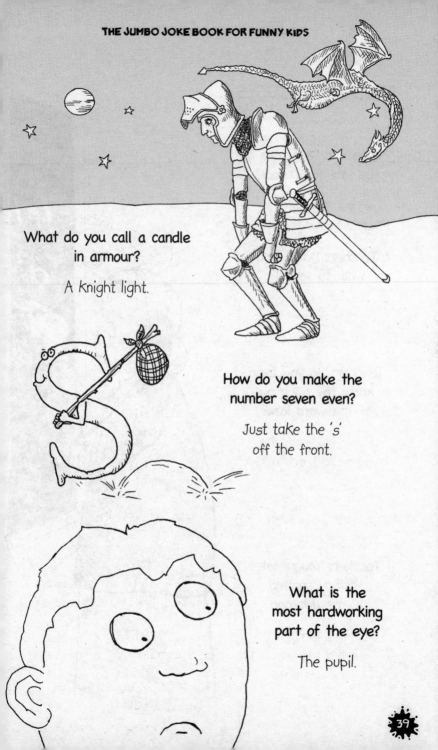

What do you call a candle
in armour?

A Knight light.

How do you make the
number seven even?

Just take the 's'
off the front.

What is the
most hardworking
part of the eye?

The pupil.

# EXCUSES, EXCUSES ...

Teacher: Why are
you late for school?

Pupil: My mum's
car broke down.

Teacher: Don't you
walk to school?

Teacher: Do you even
know the meaning
of the word late?

Pupil: No – maybe
you could teach me?

Teacher: You're late.
History started
10 minutes ago.

Pupil: I thought it
started thousands
of years ago.

**Teacher: You're late. Don't you have a watch?**

Pupil: I threw it out of the window so time would fly.

**Teacher: You're late again.**

Pupil: You mean I have to be on time every day?

**Teacher: What's your excuse this time?**

Pupil: My shoes got a puncture.

41

# Silly, Strange Stuff

**What kind of androids do you get in the Arctic?**

**Snow-bots.**

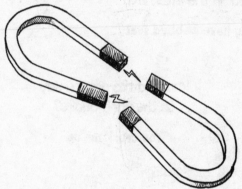

**What did one magnet say to the other?**

**"I find you very attractive."**

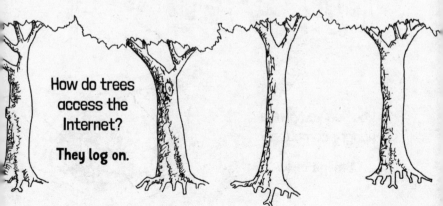

**How do trees access the Internet?**

**They log on.**

43

Why are penguins so
good on the Internet?

**They have webbed feet.**

What did the ground say
to the earthquake?

**"You crack me up."**

What do you give a
hungry computer?

**A mega-byte.**

What did one romantic volcano say to the other?

**"I lava you."**

What is the centre of gravity?

**The letter 'v'.**

Why can't a T. rex clap?

**Because it's extinct.**

45

What do you get if
you cross a river
and a stream?

**Wet.**

What kind of tree is
good at maths?

**Geo-me-tree.**

Why might grass
cut you?

**It's full of blades.**

Why do toadstools grow so closely together?

**They don't need mush-room.**

How do you know if the sea's friendly?

**Say "hello" and it'll wave back.**

What lies at the bottom of the ocean and shakes?

**A nervous wreck.**

**Where does a river put its money?**

**In the river bank.**

**Which insect runs away from everything?**

**A flea.**

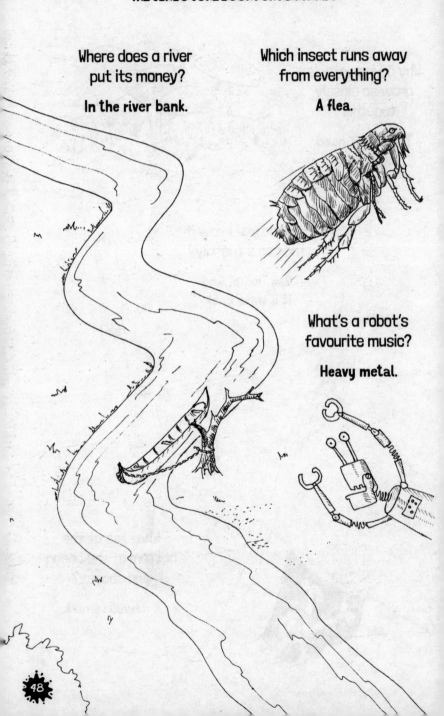

**What's a robot's favourite music?**

**Heavy metal.**

48

What do you say
to a dead robot?

**Rust in peace.**

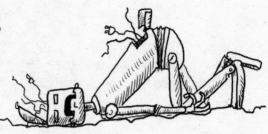

Why do bees hum?

**Because they forgot
the words.**

What do you call a
frog with no legs?

**Un-hoppy.**

If a tree could hug you ...

... it wood.

What has a bottom
at the top?

**Your legs.**

Why are worms
always so
frightened?

**They have
no backbone.**

What's a tornado's favourite game?

**Twister.**

Why did the computer keep sneezing?

**It had a virus.**

What do you get when you cross a vampire and a snowman?

**Frost-bite.**

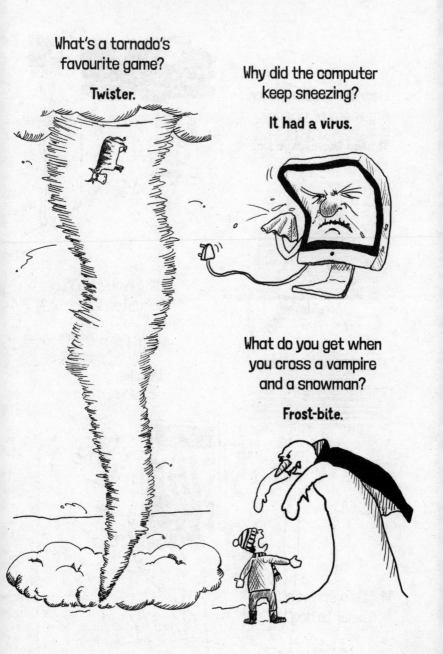

51

How did the computer
get out of prison?

It used the escape key.

Why would you take a
laptop for a run?

To jog its memory.

What's a scientist's
favourite dog?

A lab.

What travels the
fastest – heat or cold?

**Heat – because you
can catch cold.**

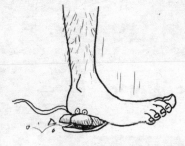

Why did the
computer squeak?

**Someone stepped
on its mouse.**

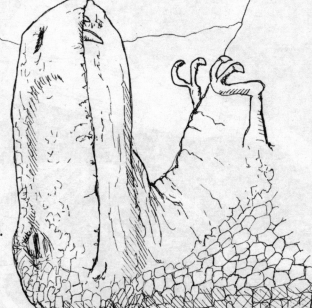

Where do
dinosaurs
sunbathe?

**At the dino-shore.**

Out Of This World

**Why did the alien
go to the doctor?**

It looked a little green.

**What do you get when
you cross an alien with
something white
and fluffy?**

A Martian-mallow.

**What do Martians serve
their dinner on?**

Flying saucers.

**Why did the star go to school?**

To get brighter.

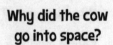

**How do you know when the Moon has had enough to eat?**

When it's a full Moon.

**Why did the cow go into space?**

To see the Mooooo-n.

**What do planets like to read?**

Comet books.

**What's an astronaut's favourite key on the keyboard?**

The space bar.

**What do you call an alien starship that weeps?**

A crying saucer.

**Which planet has the most bling?**

Saturn, because it has rings.

**Why was the restaurant on the Moon empty?**

Because it had no atmosphere.

**What happened when the girl stayed up all night looking for the Sun?**

It suddenly dawned on her.

### What did Earth say to the other planets?

"You guys have no life."

### What did the alien say to the gardener?

"Take me to your weeder."

### What do aliens like to drink?

Gravi-tea.

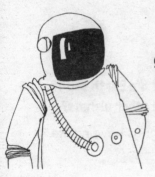

**What do you get if you cross a wizard and an astronaut?**

A flying sorcerer.

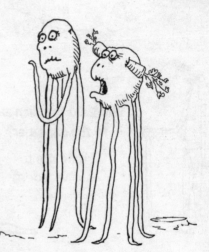

**What do you call an alien with carrots in its ears?**

Anything you want, it can't hear you!

**What kind of stars wear sunglasses?**

Movie stars.

**What did the astronaut find in his kitchen?**

An Unidentified Frying Object.

**What's an astronaut's favourite board game?**

Moon-opoly.

**What do astronauts spread on their toast?**

Mars-malade.

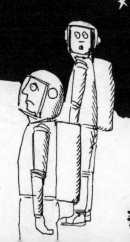

**What time do astronauts eat?**

Launch time.

**How do you get in touch with someone on Saturn?**

Just give them a ring.

**How does the Solar System keep its trousers up?**

With an asteroid belt.

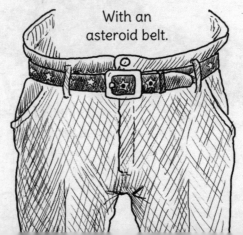

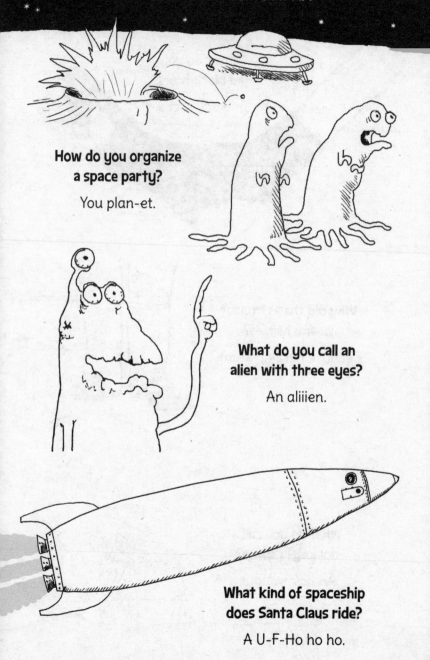

**How do you organize
a space party?**

You plan-et.

**What do you call an
alien with three eyes?**

An aliiien.

**What kind of spaceship
does Santa Claus ride?**

A U-F-Ho ho ho.

**Where do you find black holes?**

In black socks.

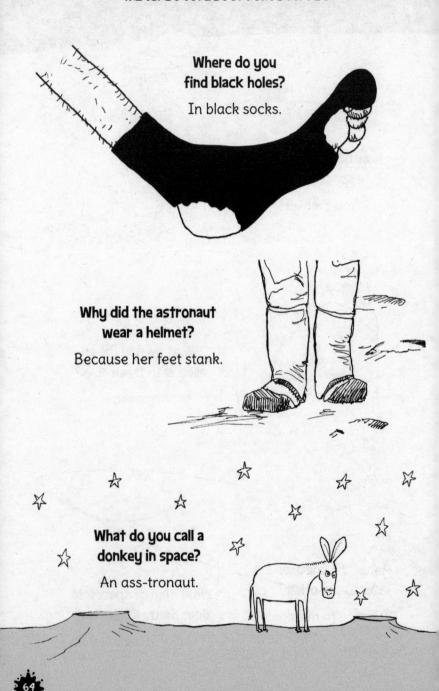

**Why did the astronaut wear a helmet?**

Because her feet stank.

**What do you call a donkey in space?**

An ass-tronaut.

**What's a cow's favourite part of space?**

The Milky Way.

**Why did Mickey Mouse go into space?**

He was looking for Pluto.

**What did one alien say to the other?**

"It's nice to meteor."

**What do you do if you see an alien in a crowd?**

Give it some space.

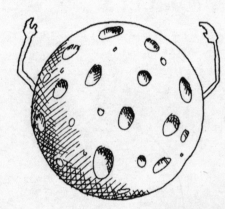

**Why doesn't the Moon need a haircut?**

It has no 'air.

**Did you hear the joke about space?**

It was out of this world.

# Animal Roarers

**Why did the chicken cross the playground?**

To get to the other slide.

**What does a cat say when it gets hurt?**

"Me-owww."

**How does a lion like its steak?**

ROAR!

68

**Knock Knock!**

Who's there?

**Amos.**

Amos, who?

**Amos-quito!**

**Knock Knock!**

Who's there?

**Anna.**

Anna, who?

**Anna-ther mosquito!**

**What colour
do cats love?**

Purrrr-ple.

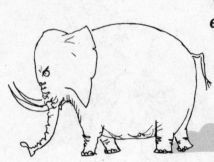

**What happened to the elephant who ran away with the circus?**

He packed his trunk and left.

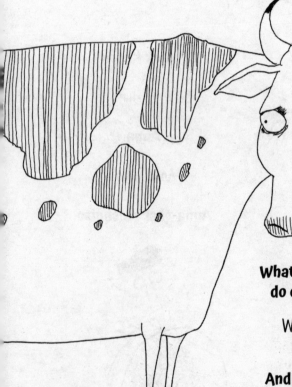

**What do cows like to do on a weekend?**

Watch moo-vies.

**And where do cows watch them?**

MooTube.

## What do you call a fly without wings?

A walk.

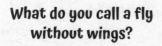

## What has eight arms and tells the time?

A clock-topus.

## How do snails keep their shells shiny?

Snail varnish.

**What do you call a cat in the desert?**

Sandy Claws.

**Why did the octopus beat the shark in a fight?**

Because it was well-armed.

**What do you call a bear with no teeth?**

A gummy bear.

**My cat was just
sick on the carpet ...**

... I don't think it
was feline well.

**Why did the lion
lose the race?**

Because he was
racing a cheetah.

**Why are frogs so happy?**

They eat whatever
bugs them.

**How many tickles does it take to make an octopus laugh?**

Ten-tickles.

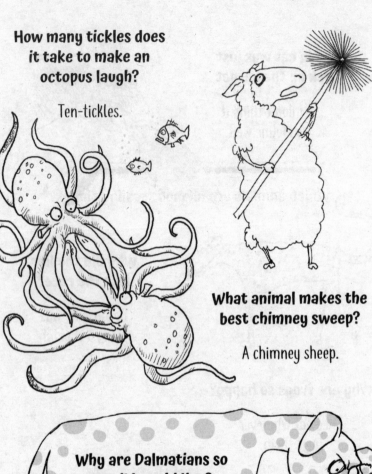

**What animal makes the best chimney sweep?**

A chimney sheep.

**Why are Dalmatians so terrible at hiding?**

They're always spotted.

**What do you call a fish with no eyes?**

A fsh.

**Which animals are always stealing things?**

Crook-odiles.

**What do you call a pig that does karate?**

A pork chop.

**What do you call a sleeping bull?**

A bulldozer.

**Where do rabbits go after they get married?**

On their bunny-moon.

**What do you call a lazy kangaroo?**

A pouch potato.

## Why did the snake cross the road?

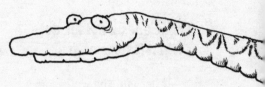

To get to the other sssssside.

## What do you call a lion's reflection?

A copycat.

## What's black and white and delivers milk?

A panda on a milk round.

**What does a spider do when it gets angry?**

It goes up the wall.

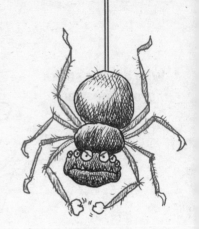

**Why don't lobsters give to charity?**

They're shellfish.

**Why do French people eat snails?**

They don't like fast food.

**What do you get if you cross a fish and an elephant?**

Swimming trunks.

**Why did the bunny go to hospital?**

For a hop-eration.

**What do you call a blind deer?**

No eye deer.

# Random Rib Ticklers

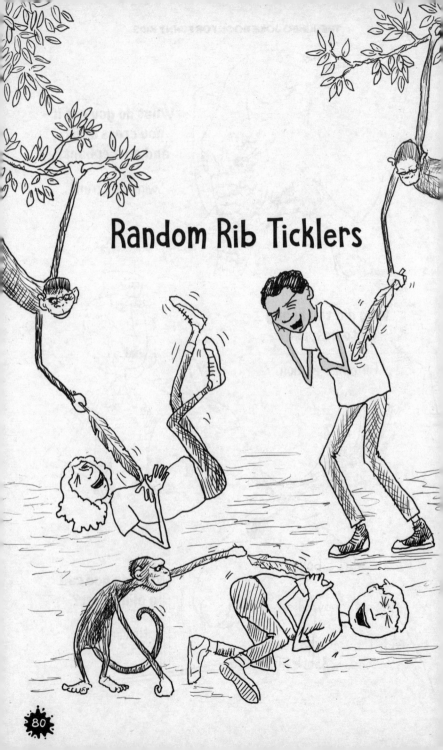

What's brown
and sticky?

A stick.

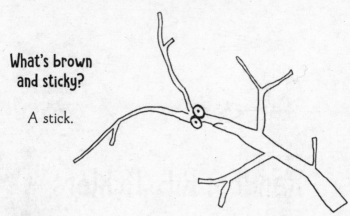

What did the dentist
say to the pirate?

Say "arrrghh."

Knock Knock!

Who's there?

A little boy.

A little boy, who?

A little boy who can't
reach the doorbell!

What did the man say when
he walked into a pole?

"Ouch!"

What falls from the sky
but never gets hurt?

Rain.

What do you call cheese
that isn't yours?

Nacho cheese.

What's orange and
sounds like a parrot?

A carrot.

What did the finger
say to the thumb?

"I'm in glove with you."

Why did the little boy
throw the toast out
of the window?

He wanted to see
the butter fly.

What do you call a girl
with one leg shorter
than the other?

Eileen.

I used to be afraid
of hurdles ...

... but I got over it.

How do trees
make friends?

They branch out.

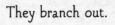

**Don't you feel sorry for shopping trolleys?**

They're always getting pushed around.

**Why did the human cannonball leave their job?**

They got fired.

**What do clouds have on under their clothes?**

Thunder-wear.

85

What kind of coat is wet
when you put it on?

A coat of paint.

Why are pirates pirates?

Because they arrrghh.

Why was 6 afraid of 7?

Because 7 ate 9.

**What did one snowman say to the other?**

"Can you smell carrots?"

**Two fish are in a tank ...**

... one says to the other, "I have no idea how to drive this thing."

**Why don't monsters eat clowns?**

Because they taste funny.

Knock Knock!

Who's there?

**Cows go.**

Cows go, who?

**No, silly – cows go moo!**

**What did the the doctor say to the boy with chocolate hanging out of his nose?**

"I don't think you're eating it properly."

**What's small, purple and dangerous?**

A grape with a water pistol.

**What did the duck ask for at the end of a meal?**

The bill.

**Which side of a leopard has the most spots?**

The outside.

**What's the difference between broccoli and bogeys?**

Children don't like eating broccoli.

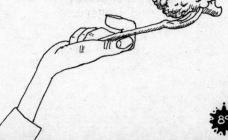

**What do you call a
blind dinosaur?**

Do-you-think-
he-saw-us.

**Where do generals
keep their armies?**

Up their sleevies.

**How do fish
weigh themselves?**

They have scales.

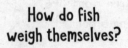

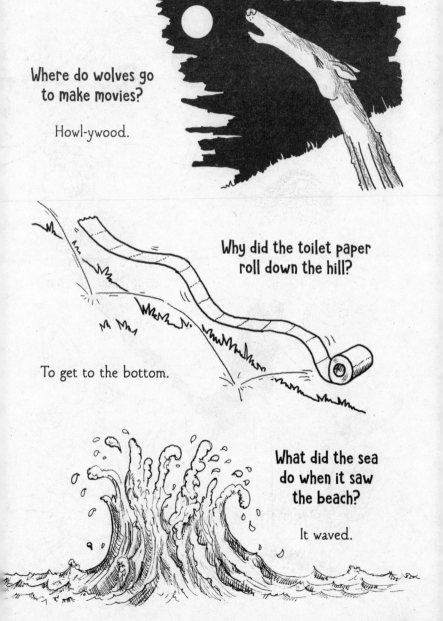

Where do wolves go
to make movies?

Howl-ywood.

Why did the toilet paper
roll down the hill?

To get to the bottom.

What did the sea
do when it saw
the beach?

It waved.

Foody Fun

**What do you serve but never eat?**

A tennis ball.

**Why did the man get fired from the orange juice factory?**

Because he couldn't concentrate.

**Why is the sea so strong?**

It has a lot of mussels.

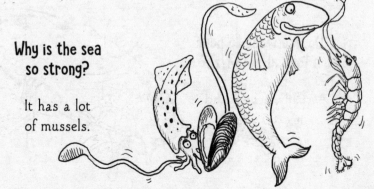

## Why did the biscuit cry?

Because his father
was a wafer so long.

## I cut my finger
## chopping cheese ...

... but I think I have
grater problems.

## Do you want to hear
## a joke about pizza?

Actually, never mind –
it's too cheesy.

**What's red and invisible?**

No tomatoes.

**Why did the tomato turn red?**

Because it saw the salad dressing.

**What do you get when you ask a lemon for help?**

Lemon-aid.

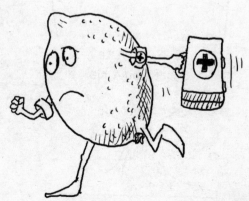

What do you call a fish with a tie?

So-fish-ticated.

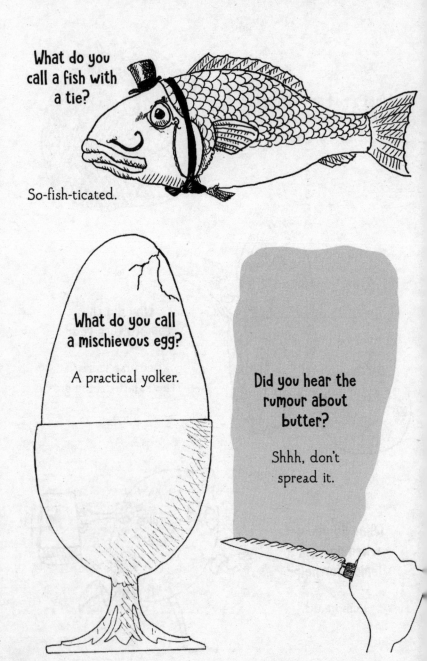

What do you call a mischievous egg?

A practical yolker.

Did you hear the rumour about butter?

Shhh, don't spread it.

**Why did the banana go to the doctor?**

It wasn't peeling well.

**What kind of nut always seems to have a cold?**

Cashew.

**Which day of the week do eggs dread?**

Fry-day.

Two muffins were in the oven. One said, "Wow, it's hot in here."

The other said, "Wow, a talking muffin."

**What do sea monsters eat?**
Fish and ships.

**What cheese is made backwards?**

Edam.

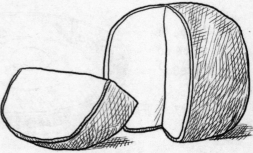

**What do you get if you cross a snake and a pie?**

A pie-thon.

**What kind of shoe can you make from a banana?**

A slipper.

**What do cats eat for breakfast?**

Mice crispies.

**What kind of key opens a banana?**

A mon-key.

**Why did the pepper put a jumper on?**

It was a little chilli.

**What do dogs eat at the movies?**

Pup-corn.

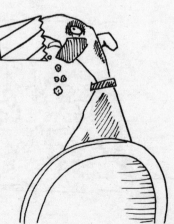

What did one
plate say to the
other plate?

"Dinner is on me."

What do computers
love to eat?

Microchips.

Why did the biscuit
go to the doctor?

Because it felt
crumb-y.

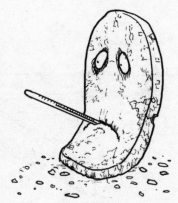

What does bread
do on its day off?

Loaf around.

Why did the carrot like to
hang out with the mushroom?

He was a fun-guy.

What vegetables
do sailors hate?

Leeks.

**Why did the pie go to the dentist?**

It needed a filling.

**Where do milkshakes come from?**

Nervous cows.

**What do you call someone who steals a pig?**

A ham-burglar.

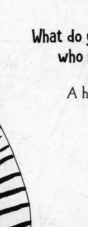

Waiter, Waiter! Do you serve fish?

Of course, we serve anyone.

Waiter, Waiter! Do you have frogs' legs?

No, Sir, that's just the way I walk.

Waiter, Waiter! There's a twig in my soup.

Hold on, I'll get the branch manager.

Waiter, Waiter!
There's a slug
in my salad.

I'm sorry, I didn't
know you were
a vegetarian.

Waiter, Waiter!
This coffee tastes
like mud.

I'm not surprised -
it was ground
this morning.

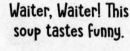

Waiter, Waiter! This
soup tastes funny.

Why aren't you
laughing then?

Waiter, Waiter!
This egg is bad.

Don't blame me,
I only laid the table.

Waiter, Waiter! What's
this in my salad?

I really couldn't say,
all bugs look the
same to me.

Waiter, Waiter!
I can't eat this.
Please get the manager.

It's no use, the manager
won't eat it either.

### Waiter, Waiter! My water's cloudy.

You're mistaken, Madam. That's dirt on the glass.

### Waiter, Waiter! This cheese is full of holes.

It could be worse – it used to be full of maggots.

### Waiter, Waiter! Will my pizza be long?

No, it will be round.

**How can you see flying saucers?**

Trip up a waiter.

**Waiter, Waiter! What can you suggest for a quick snack?**

Runner beans.

**Waiter, Waiter! I can't eat this meat — it's crawling with maggots.**

Quick, run to the other end of the table and you can catch it as it goes by.

Waiter: Would you
like your coffee black?

Customer: What other
colours do you have?

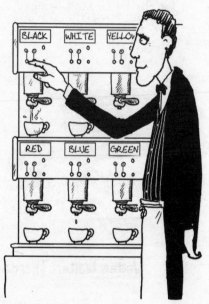

Waiter, Waiter!
What's this I'm eating?

It looks like small
chunks of chicken and
large chunks of vegetables.

Waiter, Waiter! I'd
like to know what's in
today's stew.

No, Madam, you
wouldn't.

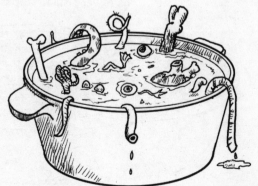

**Waiter:** You haven't touched your jelly.

Customer: No, I'm waiting for the fly to stop using it as a trampoline.

**Did you hear about the worst restaurant in the world?**

It was so bad that flies went there to lose weight.

**Waiter, Waiter! There's a mosquito in my soup.**

Don't worry, mosquitoes have very small appetites.

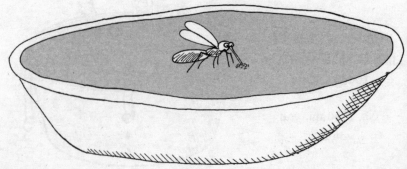

**Waiter, Waiter! Is there soup on the menu?**

Yes, Sir, but I can clean it off if you like.

**How did the waiter get an electric shock?**

He stepped on a bun and a currant went up his leg.

**Waiter, Waiter! What do you call this?**

Shepherd's pie, Madam.

**Ooh, I've never eaten a shepherd before.**

Waiter, Waiter!
I don't like cheese
with holes.

Well, just eat the cheese
and leave the holes on
the side of your plate.

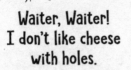

Waiter, Waiter! I thought
there was a choice for
lunch today.

There is, Sir.

No there isn't, there's
only cheese pie.

You can choose to
eat it or leave it.

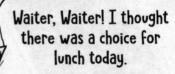

Waiter, Waiter! This fish
doesn't taste as good
as it did last week.

That's odd. It's
the same fish.

# Dopey Dinosaurs and Big Beasts

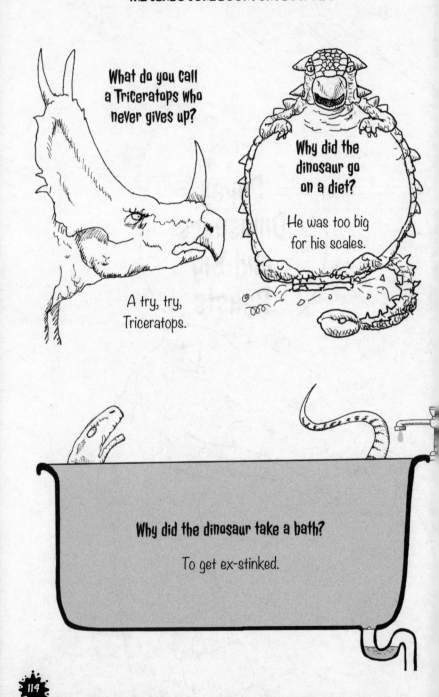

What do you call a Triceratops who never gives up?

A try, try, Triceratops.

Why did the dinosaur go on a diet?

He was too big for his scales.

Why did the dinosaur take a bath?

To get ex-stinked.

**Why are dinosaurs no longer around?**

Because their eggs stink.

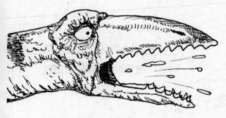

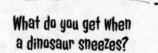

**What do you get when a dinosaur sneezes?**

Out of the way.

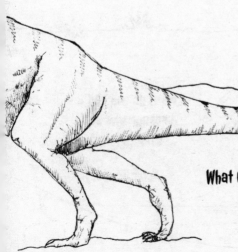

**What came after dinosaurs?**

Their tails.

How does a T. rex
say hello?

"Pleased to eat you."

What has a spiked tail,
armour plates and
8 wheels?

A Stegosaurus
on roller skates.

What do you call a
dinosaur who won't
stop talking?

A dino-bore.

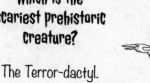

### Which is the scariest prehistoric creature?

The Terror-dactyl.

### Why can't you hear a Pterodactyl on the toilet?

Because it has a silent 'p'.

### What do you call a dinosaur who knows lots of words?

A Thesaurus.

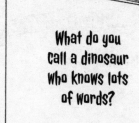

**How do you ask a dinosaur for a hot drink?**

"Tea, Rex?"

**What do you call a dinosaur that's a noisy sleeper?**

A Bronto-snorus.

**Who makes prehistoric clothes?**

A dino-sewer.

**What do you get if you cross a pig with a dinosaur?**

Jurassic Pork.

**What do you call a sleeping dinosaur?**

A dino-snore.

Z Z Z Z Z

**Where does a T. rex sit when it comes to stay?**

Anywhere it wants to.

**Why did the dragon keep
burning his fingers?**

He covered his mouth
every time he coughed.

**What do you give
a seasick dragon?**

A very large, fireproof bag.

**Did you hear about the dragons
who could play the piano?**

They really knew their scales.

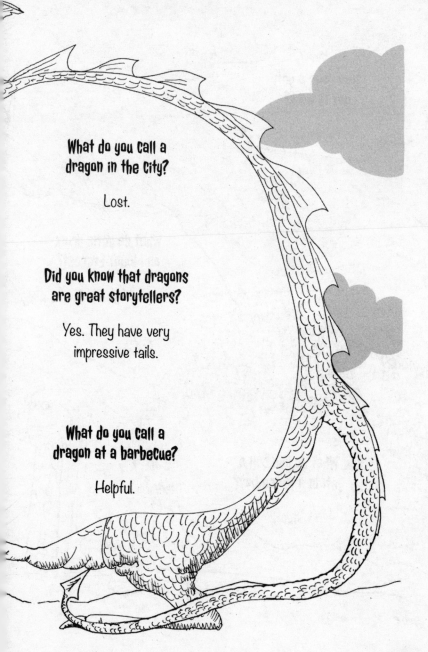

**What do you call a dragon in the City?**

Lost.

**Did you know that dragons are great storytellers?**

Yes. They have very impressive tails.

**What do you call a dragon at a barbecue?**

Helpful.

How does a yeti
get to work?

By icicle.

What do yetis drink
on Mount Everest?

High tea.

What do you call a
yeti in a phone box?

Stuck.

**Where are yetis found?**

They're so big, they're hardly ever lost.

**What do snow monsters eat for dinner?**

Spag-yeti.

**How did the yeti feel when he had the flu?**

Abominable.

# Side Splitters

**What happens to frogs
that break down?**

They get toad away.

**Why did the ram
crash his car?**

He didn't see
the ewe-turn.

**What goes
"aaab aaab"?**

A reversing sheep.

125

## Which dog sailed around the world?

Christo-fur Columbus.

## What do you get if you cross a lake with a leaky boat?

About halfway.

## How did the two octopus friends walk along the road?

Arm in arm in arm in arm in arm in arm in arm in arm.

**What buzzes, is black and yellow and sits at the bottom of the sea?**

A bee in a submarine.

**How do fish get to school?**

By octo-bus.

**Where can you buy a cheap yacht?**

In a sail.

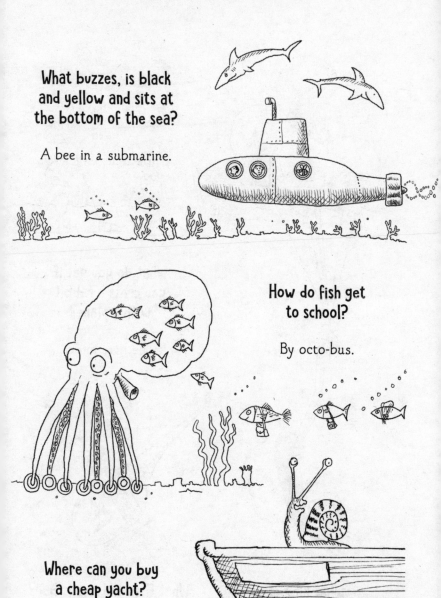

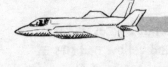

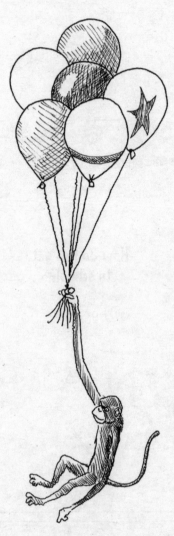

**What do you get if you cross a rabbit with a plane?**

The hare-force.

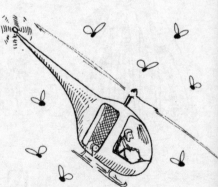

**What kind of monkey can fly?**

A hot-air baboon.

**What flies and smells bad?**

A smelly-copter.

How do you know
that planes are afraid
of the dark?

They always leave
their landing lights on.

What do you get if
you cross a big ape
with a plane?

King Kong-corde.

How do nits
travel abroad?

On British
Hair-ways.

## What do pigs drive?

Pig-up trucks.

## Why did the elephant put her trunk across the road?

To trip up the ants.

## What do you get if you cross a broomstick with a motorcycle?

A broom, broom broomstick.

## When does your hamster drive your car?

When you're not looking.

## Why are police officers so strong?

Because they hold up traffic.

## Did you hear about the first deer to pass his driving test?

He really bucked the trend.

## What's the slowest horse in the world?

A clothes horse.

## Why don't elephants ride bikes?

They don't have a thumb to ring the bell.

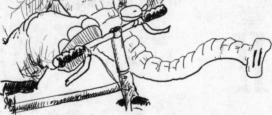

## Where do mice put their boats?

At the hickory dickory dock.

I'm giving away a free parachute ...

... no strings attached.

**Why did the frog cross the road?**

To see what was hoppening on the other side.

**What do you call a stupid boat?**

An idi-yacht.

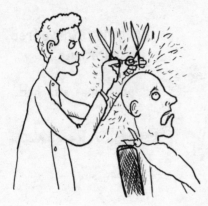

**Why are barbers such good drivers?**

Because they know all the shortcuts.

**How do fleas travel?**

They itch-hike.

**How do lobsters get to work?**

In a taxi-crab.

What did the red traffic light say to the green traffic light?

"Don't look, I'm changing."

Why are geese bad drivers?

They honk all the time.

What's the difference between a bus driver and a cold?

One knows the stops and the other stops the nose.

## Where do astronauts leave their spaceships?

At parking meteors.

## What was the first animal in space?

The cow that jumped over the moon.

## What did the astronaut say when he farted on the moon?

"I Apollo-gize."

Doctor, Doctor!
I feel like a spoon.

Sit still and don't stir.

Doctor, Doctor!
I keep seeing pink spots.

Have you seen
an optician?

No, just pink spots.

Doctor, Doctor!
People tell me I'm
a wheelbarrow.

Don't let people
push you around.

**Doctor, Doctor!
I feel like an apple.**

We really must get
to the core of this.

**Doctor, Doctor!
How can I make my
cough better?**

Practice, practice, practice.

**Doctor, Doctor!
I think I'm invisible.**

I'm afraid I can't
see you today.

Doctor, Doctor! What's that pain in my stomach?

You have acute appendicitis.

I came here to be treated, not flattered.

What did one tooth say to the other?

"Get your cap on, the dentist is taking us out today."

Doctor, Doctor! How do I stop my nose from running?

Stick out one foot and trip it up.

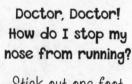

141

Doctor, Doctor! Everyone thinks I'm a liar.

I don't believe you.

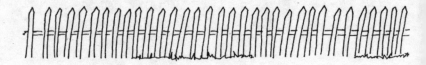

Doctor, Doctor! I think I'm turning into a fence.

Well, don't let that come between us.

Doctor, Doctor! I can't get to sleep.

Well, sit on the edge of your bed and you'll soon drop off.

**Doctor, Doctor! I keep thinking I'm a flea.**

I thought you looked a little jumpy.

**Doctor, Doctor! I think I'm a crocodile.**

Well, there's no need to snap at me.

**Doctor: Have your eyes ever been checked?**

Patient: No, they've always been brown.

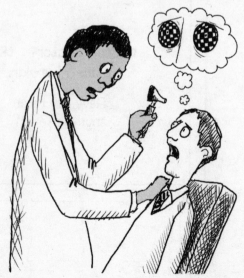

Doctor, Doctor!
What did the X-ray
of my head show?

Nothing at all.

Doctor, Doctor! I think
I've lost my memory.

When did this happen?

When did what happen?

Doctor, Doctor! I think
I am a burglar.

Have you taken
anything for it?

Doctor, Doctor!
I keep thinking there
are two of me.

One at a time, please.

Doctor, Doctor! I think
I'm a vampire.

Necks, please!

What did one ear say
to the other ear?

"Between us we
have brains."

**Why did the pillow go to the doctor?**

He was feeling all stuffed up.

**Doctor, Doctor! I think you're a bell.**

Take these pills and if they don't work, give me a ring.

**Doctor, Doctor! I feel like a sheep.**

That's baaaaad.

**Why did the doctor lose his temper?**

Because he didn't have any patients.

**Doctor, Doctor! I feel like a biscuit.**

Oh, crumbs!

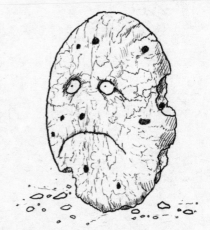

**Did you hear the one about the germ?**

Never mind, I don't want to spread it around.

How do you make
a tissue dance?

Put a little boogie in it.

If you were a bogey ...

... I'd pick you first.

What monster sits on
the end of your finger?

The bogeyman.

**What did one flea say to the other?**

"Shall we walk or take the cat?"

**How do you tell which end of a worm is which?**

Tickle the middle and see which end laughs.

**What's worse than finding a maggot in your apple?**

Finding half a maggot!

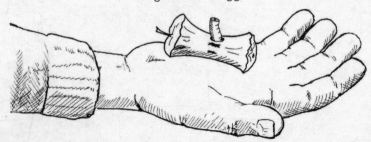

**Why did the glow-worm sit in a bucket of water?**

You would too if your bum was on fire.

**What do you call a spider with no legs?**

A raisin.

**How do you find out which end of a worm is which?**

Drop it in a glass of lemonade and see which end burps.

Which vegetables are found in the toilet?

Leeks and peas.

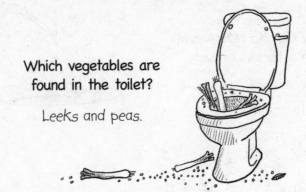

What happened when the chef found a daddy longlegs in the salad?

It became a daddy shortlegs.

What is hairy and coughs?

A coconut with a cold.

What's got four
legs and an arm?

A crocodile
eating dinner.

What does the Queen
do when she burps?

Issues a royal pardon.

What do you call
a bee in a bun?

A hum-burger.

What do you get if
you cross a skunk with
a pair of rubber boots?

Smelly wellies.

It is well known that
exercise kills germs.

But how on earth
do you get germs
to exercise?

Why does a giraffe
have such a long neck?

Because it has smelly feet.

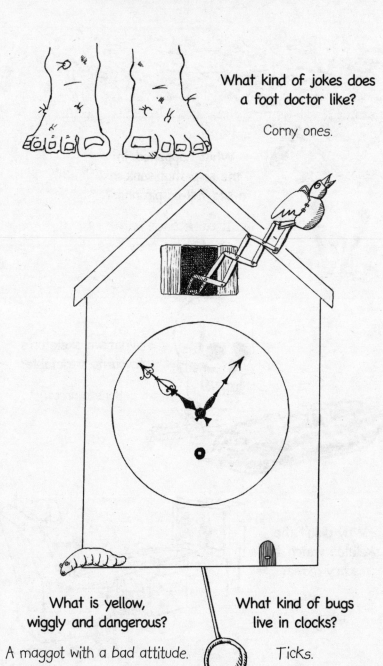

What kind of jokes does
a foot doctor like?

Corny ones.

What is yellow,
wiggly and dangerous?

A maggot with a bad attitude.

What kind of bugs
live in clocks?

Ticks.

What happened to
the ship that sank in
a sea full of piranhas?

It came back with
a skeleton crew.

What's a skeleton's
favourite vegetable?

Bone marrow.

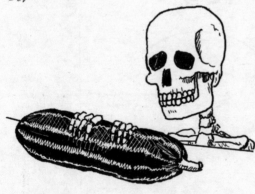

Why didn't the
skeleton watch the
scary movie?

It didn't have
the guts.

What's invisible and
smells like carrots?

Bunny burps.

Why did the man
become a weather
presenter?

He was good
at passing wind.

How many farts
does it take to
empty a room?

A phew.

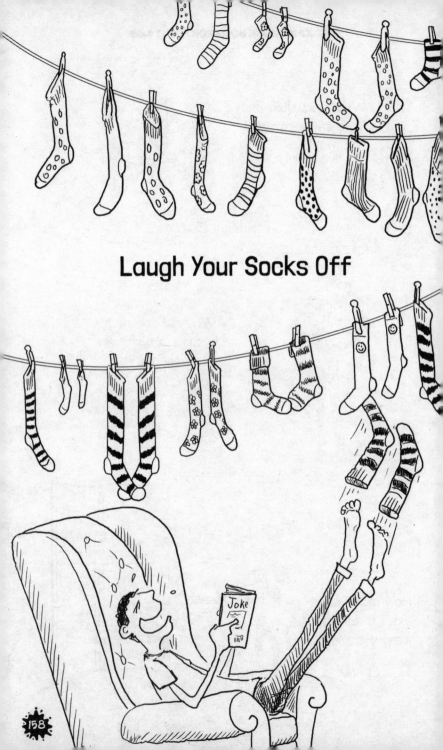

# Laugh Your Socks Off

What did one pig say
to the other?

"Let's be pen pals."

Why do cows lie
down when it's cold?

To keep each
udder warm.

What do sheep do on sunny days?

Have a baa-baa-cue.

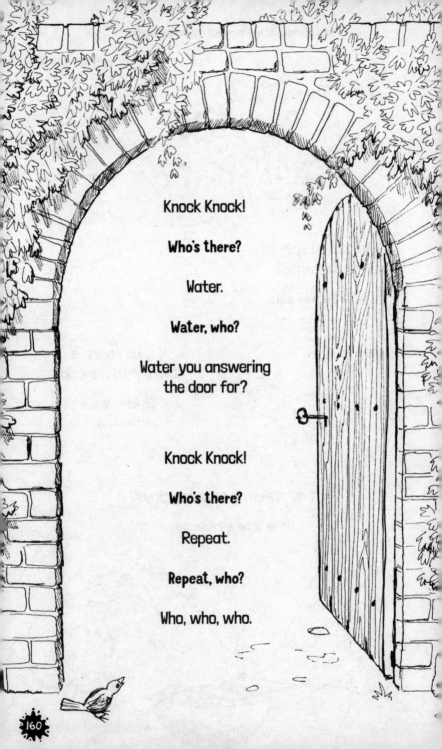

Knock Knock!

**Who's there?**

Water.

**Water, who?**

Water you answering
the door for?

Knock Knock!

**Who's there?**

Repeat.

**Repeat, who?**

Who, who, who.

Knock Knock!

Who's there?

Goat.

Goat, who?

Goat to the front
door and find out.

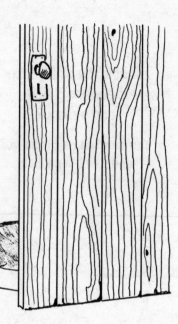

Knock Knock!

Who's there?

Archie.

Archie, who?

Bless you.

What's the difference
between a fish
and a piano?

You can tune a piano but
you can't tuna fish.

What do you call
a failed pelican?

A peli-can't.

Where do seagulls invest
their money?

In the stork market.

What do you call a surgeon
with eight arms?

**A doctor-pus.**

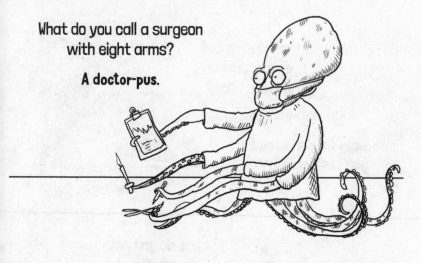

What was the speed
limit in ancient Egypt?

**Forty Niles
per hour.**

What did one rock pool say to the other?

**"Show us your mussels."**

163

What do you call
a woodpecker
with no beak?

**A headbanger.**

What do you get
if you cross a dog
with an aardvark?

**An aard-bark.**

How do you
count cows?

**With a
cow-culator.**

164

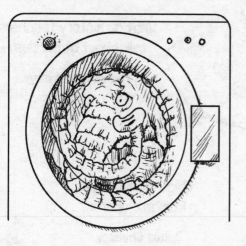

What's big and goes round and round?

**An elephant in a washing machine.**

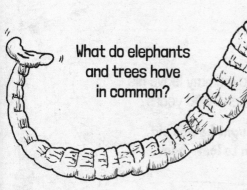

What do elephants and trees have in common?

**They both have big trunks.**

What's the difference between an elephant and a biscuit?

**You can't dip an elephant in your tea.**

What do history teachers talk about at parties?

**The good old days.**

Which mouse was a Roman emperor?

**Julius Cheeser.**

Why did the mummy leave his tomb after 3,000 years?

**He thought he was old enough to leave home.**

Why is history so fruity?

It's full of dates.

What was the fruit that launched a thousand ships?

Melon of Troy.

Why was the mummy so tense?

She was too wound up!

Did you hear about the
mathematical plants?

**They grew
square roots.**

What kind of nut
hangs on the wall?

**A walnut.**

How do you stop an
astronaut's baby
from crying?

**You rock-et.**

If we breathe oxygen
in the daytime, what do
we breathe at night?

Night-rogen.

My dad got me
a dictionary for
my birthday ...

... I still couldn't
find the words
to thank him.

How do you cure
a shy pebble?

Make it a
little boulder.

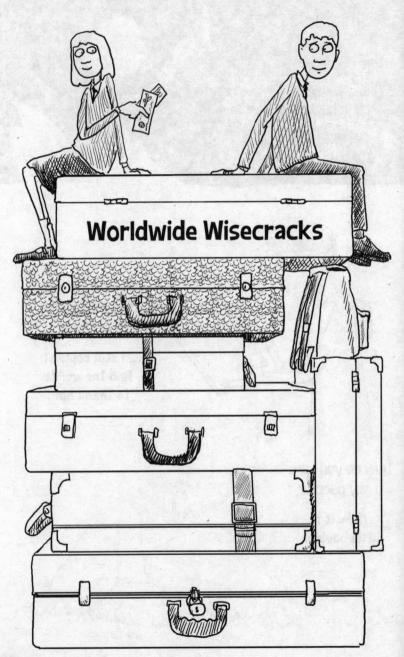

# Worldwide Wisecracks

**What is Australia's most popular fizzy drink?**

Coca-Koala.

**What do you get if you cross a kangaroo with an elephant?**

Huge holes all over Australia.

**What's the scariest part of Australia?**

The Northern Terror-tory.

**In which city can you wander around aimlessly?**

Rome.

**How do you make a Venetian blind?**

Poke him in the eye.

**What's tall, Italian and covered in pepperoni?**

The Leaning Tower of Pizza.

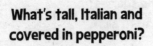

**Why should you be worried if you eat bad food in Germany?**

Because the wurst is yet to come.

**Where's the best place in the world to find sharks?**

Fin-land.

**What do you find in the middle of Japan?**

The letter 'p'.

**What do you say if someone tells a lie in South America?**

I don't Bolivia.

**Which country has the most germs?**

Germany.

**Why is it hard to learn Chinese cooking?**

You get so much home-wok.

**Where do you find Quebec?**

On a map.

**I'd love to go to The Netherlands one day ...**

... wooden shoe?

**What type of dog likes to travel the world?**

A jet-setter.

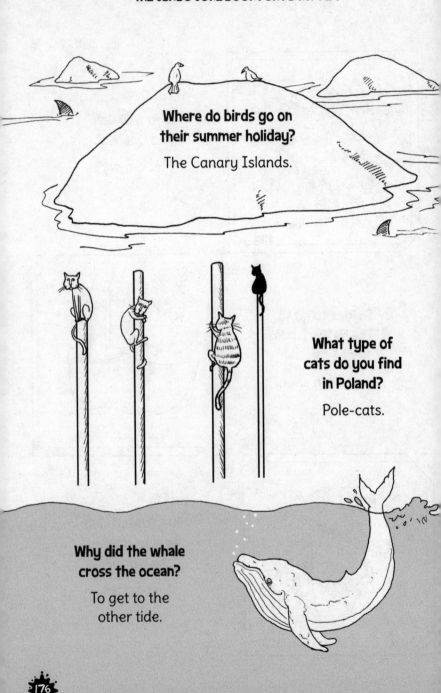

**Where do birds go on their summer holiday?**

The Canary Islands.

**What type of cats do you find in Poland?**

Pole-cats.

**Why did the whale cross the ocean?**

To get to the other tide.

**What sea is in space?**

The galax-sea.

**What kind of music can you hear in space?**

A Nep-tune.

**What do astronauts play on long journeys?**

Astro-nauts and crosses.

**Which country has
the thinnest people?**

Finland.

**What's the coldest
place in the world?**

Chile.

**In which country
are you most likely
to slip and fall over?**

Greece.

**Why is Mount Everest a good listener?**

There are so many mountain-ears on it.

**How do you find out what the weather's like at the top of a mountain?**

You climate.

**Why is it hard to talk to a goat?**

Because they're always butting in.

# Brain Bogglers

What has hands but can't clap?

A clock.

I'm not alive, but I have five fingers. What am I?

A glove.

What begins with an 'e', ends with an 'e', has an 'e' in the middle, but has only one letter?

An envelope.

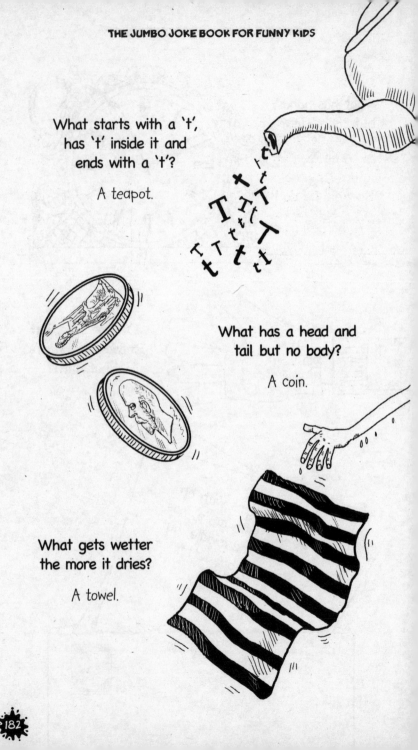

What starts with a 't',
has 't' inside it and
ends with a 't'?

A teapot.

What has a head and
tail but no body?

A coin.

What gets wetter
the more it dries?

A towel.

A cowboy rode in to town on Friday, stayed for three days, then left on Friday. How did he do it?

His horse's name was Friday.

What comes once in a minute, twice in a moment, but never in a thousand years?

The letter 'm'.

What is at the end of the rainbow?

The letter 'w'.

What's full of
holes but still
holds water?

A sponge.

Tom's mother had four
children. She named the
first child Monday, the
second Tuesday, and
the third Wednesday.
What is the name of
the fourth child?

Tom, because Tom's mother
only had four children.

What can you hold
without touching it?

Your breath.

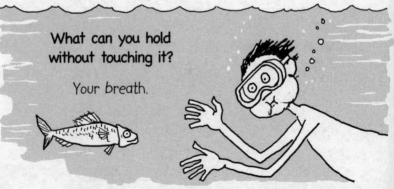

What goes up as rain comes down?

An umbrella.

When I point up, it's bright. When I point down, it's dark. What am I?

A light switch.

What has an eye but cannot see?

A needle.

What has four
legs and two arms
but no head?

An armchair.

I travel around
the world but only
stay in one corner.
What am I?

A stamp.

What has 13 hearts
but is never alive?

A pack of cards.

I'm as hard as a rock but melt in
hot water. What am I?

An ice cube.

I can hold lots of
food, but I can't eat
anything. What am I?

A fridge.

What clever invention
lets you walk
through walls?

A door.

You have a bucket filled with sand. It's too heavy to carry. What can you put in your bucket that will make it lighter and easier to carry?

A hole.

What is more useful to you once its broken?

An egg.

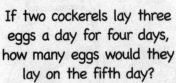

If two cockerels lay three eggs a day for four days, how many eggs would they lay on the fifth day?

None. Cockerels don't lay eggs.

What weighs
more – a kilo of
potatoes or a kilo
of balloons?

*They both weigh
the same – a kilo.*

What has
four legs but
can't walk?

*A table.*

What's easy to
catch but hard
to get rid of?

*A cold.*

**What can run
but can't walk?**

Water.

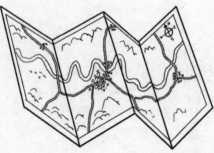

**Where can you
find cities, towns and
streets but no people?**

A map.

**What word is spelled
wrong in every
dictionary?**

The word 'wrong'.

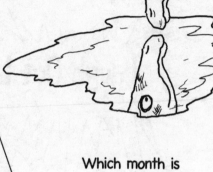

You can see me
in water but I never
get wet. What am I?

A reflection.

Which month is
the shortest?

May (it only has
three letters).

I can go through
glass without
breaking it.
What am I?

Light.

Laugh Out Loud

**What goes further the slower it goes?**

Money.

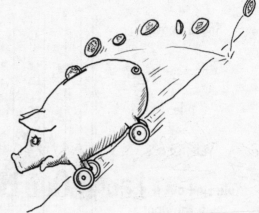

**Which pets are always found lying around the house?**

Car-pets.

**What did the teddy bear say when it was offered food?**

"No thanks, I'm stuffed."

**Knock Knock!**

Who's there?

**Yule.**

Yule, who?

**Yule find out if you open the door.**

**Knock Knock!**

Who's there?

**Cash.**

Cash, who?

**No thank you, I'm allergic to nuts.**

**Knock Knock!**

Who's there?

**Hal.**

Hal, who?

**Hal-who to you, too.**

**What do you tell a chicken who won't leave you alone?**

Just peck it in.

**What do you call a girl with a tortoise on her head?**

Shelley.

**What film do dogs like to watch?**

*The Hound of Music.*

**Why did the king go to the dentist?**

To get his teeth crowned.

**What do you give a train driver for a present?**

Platform shoes.

**What does a house wear?**

Address.

**What did Shakespeare's cat say?**

"Ta-bby or not ta-bby."

**Where did the kittens go on their school trip?**

The meow-seum.

**What's red and smells like blue paint?**

Red paint.

Knock Knock!

Who's there?

Radio.

Radio, who?

Radio not, here I come.

Did you hear about the man
who bought a paper shop?

It blew away.

Why did the tree dye its hair?

Because its roots were showing.

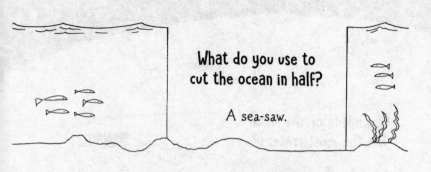

What do you use to
cut the ocean in half?

A sea-saw.

Why do dogs
run in circles?

Because it's
hard to run
in squares.

How do you spell 'hard water'
using only three letters?

'I' 'C' 'E'.

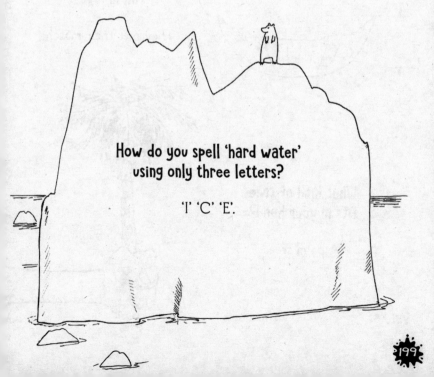

199

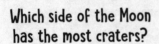

**Which side of the Moon has the most craters?**

The outside.

**Why did the candles fall in love?**

They met their match.

**What kind of tree fits in your hand?**

A palm tree.

**Why are ghosts
so bad at lying?**

You can see right
through them.

**How does the man on
the Moon cut his hair?**

E-clipse it.

**What's grey, has
four legs and a trunk?**

A mouse going on holiday.

What kind of job is it easy to stick to?

Working in a glue factory.

What did the lawyer name her daughter?

Sue.

How did the farmer mend the holes in his trousers?

With cabbage patches.

203

**What kind of shoes do spies wear?**

Sneakers.

**What do you call killer whales playing the violin?**

An orca-stra.

**What do lawyers wear to work?**

Law-suits.

**Why did the book join the police?**

He wanted to go under cover.

**Who can shave ten times a day and still have a beard?**

A barber.

**Why are chefs cruel?**

Because they whip the cream and batter the fish.

**What do you get when you cross a teacher and a vampire?**

Blood tests.

**What vegetable do librarians like?**

Quiet peas.

Shhh

**How are judges like teachers?**

They both hand out long sentences.

What time should you
go to the dentist?

Tooth-hurty.

What was the name
of the chef's son?

Stew.

What was
the name of the
chef's daughter?

Olive.

**Why did the electrician hate his job?**

Because it was shocking.

**How do scientists keep their breath fresh?**

With experi-mints.

**Knock Knock!**

Who's there?

**Police.**

Police, who?

**Police open the door, it's cold outside!**

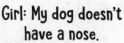

**Girl:** My dog doesn't have a nose.

**Vet:** How does it smell?

**Girl:** Awful!

**What do you call a dog that does magic?**

A Labracadabrador.

**How do you train to be a waste collector?**

You just pick it up as you go along.

209

## Why did the baker stop making donuts?

He got tired
of the hole thing.

## What's yellow and white and travels at 100 kilometres an hour?

A train driver's egg sandwich.

## Why are bakers so relaxed?

They're always
loafing around.

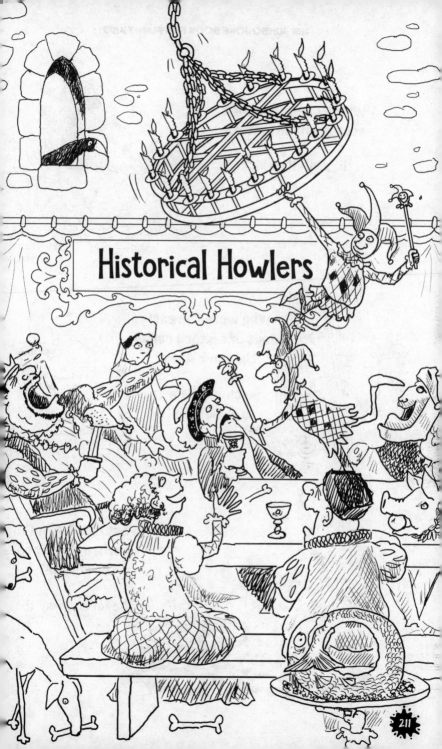

# Historical Howlers

**Which queen couldn't stop drinking water?**

Elizabeth the Thirst.

**Why were the early days of history called the Dark Ages?**

Because there were so many knights.

**What did Henry VIII do when he gained the throne?**

He sat down on it!

My teacher reminds me of history ...

... He's always repeating himself.

**Knock Knock!**

Who's there?

**Queen.**

Queen, who?

**Queen your room, it's filthy.**

**What did the executioner say to the prisoner?**

"I'm just trying to get ahead."

**What's fruity and burns?**

The Grape Fire of London.

**Who invented fractions?**

Henry the one eighth.

**Why is England such a wet country?**

Because kings and queens have reigned there for hundreds of years.

**Where was Queen Elizabeth I crowned?**

On her head.

**Why does Guy Fawkes have the best birthdays?**

His parties always go out with a bang.

**Which queen burped a lot?**

Queen Hic-toria.

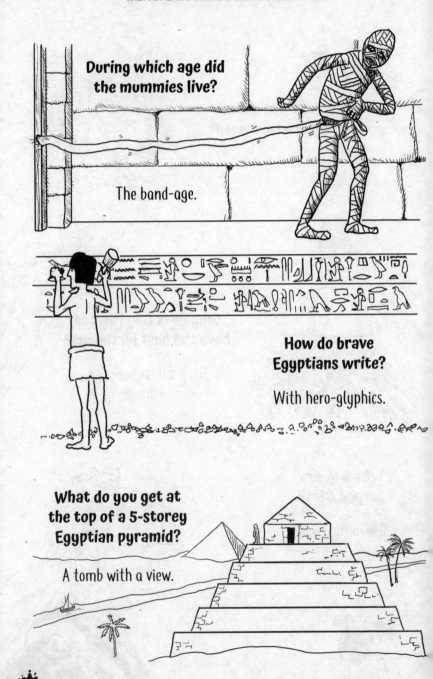

**During which age did the mummies live?**

The band-age.

**How do brave Egyptians write?**

With hero-glyphics.

**What do you get at the top of a 5-storey Egyptian pyramid?**

A tomb with a view.

**Do mummies enjoy being mummies?**

Of corpse.

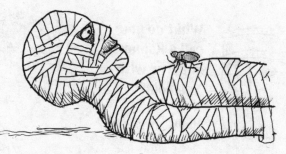

**What did Caesar say to Cleopatra?**

"Toga-ther we can rule the empire."

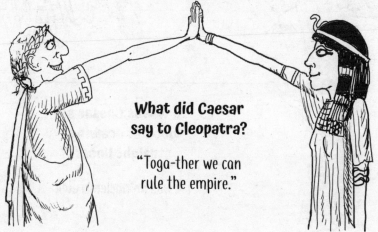

**What do ancient Egyptians say when they hear the doorbell ring?**

"Toot-and-come-in."

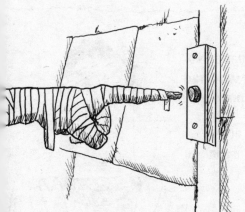

**What do you call a Roman emperor with a cold?**

Julius Sneezer.

**How was Caesar so good at drawing straight lines?**

He was an ancient ruler.

**What happened to the soldier who had his ear chopped off?**

He was never heard of again.

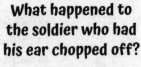

**What fish do Roman soldiers like to eat?**

Sword fish.

**How was the Roman Empire cut in half?**

With a pair of Caesars.

**Knock Knock!**

Who's there?

**Caesar.**

Caesar, who?

**Caesar! She's getting away.**

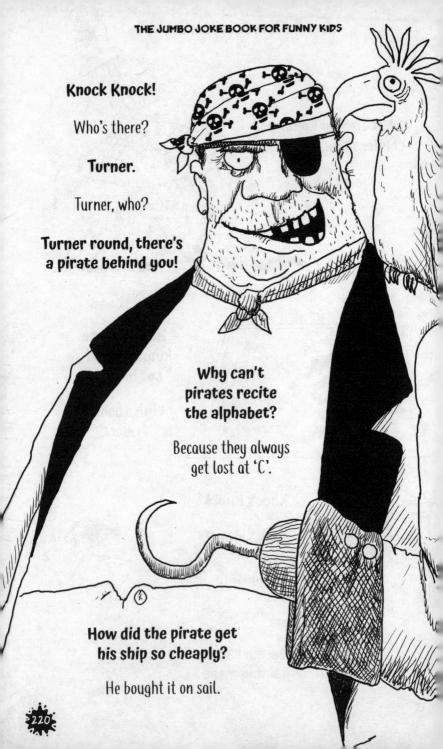

**Knock Knock!**

Who's there?

**Turner.**

Turner, who?

**Turner round, there's a pirate behind you!**

**Why can't pirates recite the alphabet?**

Because they always get lost at 'C'.

**How did the pirate get his ship so cheaply?**

He bought it on sail.

What's a pirate's favourite letter of the alphabet?

'R'rrghh!

What did the pirate say as he walked the plank?

"Water-way to go."

What do you call a pirate with four eyes?

A piiiirate.

221

**What was the most popular music in the Stone Age?**

Rock and roll.

**Why did the mammoth have a woolly coat?**

He would have looked silly in a jacket.

**What do you call a dinosaur at the bottom of the ocean?**

A Tyrannosaurus wreck.

**Caveman 1:
Why do we eat
tortoises all
the time?**

Caveman 2:
Too much fast
food is bad
for you.

**In which period of history
did no one's clothes have
any wrinkles?**

The Iron Age.

**Why did King
Arthur have a
round table?**

So he couldn't
be cornered.

Did you hear about
the kidnapping in
the park?

**They woke him up.**

What's worse than one
crocodile coming to
dinner?

**Two crocodiles coming
to dinner.**

Did you hear about the brainy
girl who ate her homework?

**She thought it was
a piece of cake.**

225

Why did the chickens
cross the road?

They thought it was
an egg-cellent idea.

What do you get when you
cross a cow with a camel?

Humpy custard.

Did you hear about the musical instrument found in the bathroom?

It was a tuba toothpaste.

What do you get when you cross a ghost with a kitten?

A scaredy cat.

What's the cleverest type of chocolate?

A smartie.

What is fast, loud
and delicious?

A rocket chip.

Did you hear about
the restaurant on
the Moon?

The food is out
of this world.

Why did the
kettle get so hot?

It wanted to
blow off steam.

What do you get when you cross
a snake with a builder?

**A boa-constructor.**

What do you call
two guys hanging
on a window?

**Kurt and Rod.**

Why did the
bacon laugh?

**The egg cracked a yolk.**

Why did the duck cross the road?

**It was the chicken's day off.**

How do you catch a school of fish?

**With bookworms.**

What do you get when you cross an elephant with a bag of crisps?

**Mashed potatoes.**

What's the difference between school dinners and a pile of slugs?

**School dinners come on a plate.**

What do you get when you cross a cow with a grass cutter?

**A lawn-mooer.**

Did you hear about the man who put on a clean pair of socks every day of the week?

**By Sunday he could hardly get his shoes on.**

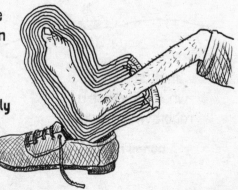

Why can't you trust
frogs with paper?

**They rip-it.**

Did you hear about
the woman who
nearly drowned in
a bowl of muesli?

**A strong currant
pulled her under.**

What do you get
when you cross a
rabbit with a frog?

**A bunny ribbit.**

What do you call
a man lying on
your doorstep?

Matt.

Waiter, Waiter! What
do you call this?

That's bean soup, Madam.

I don't care what it's
been. What is it now?

What happens when
you fill a suitcase
with toadstools?

There's not mush-room
for your holiday clothes.

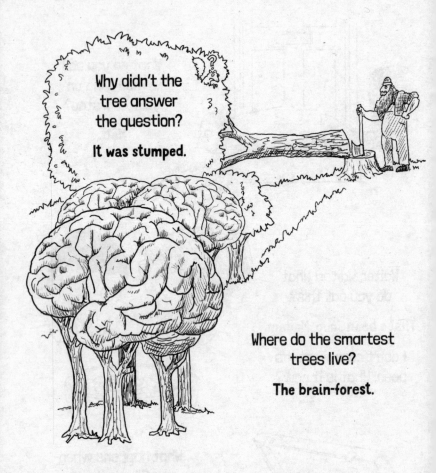

Why didn't the
tree answer
the question?

It was stumped.

Where do the smartest
trees live?

The brain-forest.

Why did the man
run around his bed?

He was trying to catch
up on his sleep.

What do you
call a rich elf?

**Welfy.**

What do you get when you
cross a cocker spaniel, a
poodle and a rooster?

**A cocker-poodle-doo.**

What do you call
two bananas?

**A pair of slippers.**

# Love and
# Laughter

What did one sheep say to the other?

"I love ewe."

Why did the owl invite her friends over?

She didn't want to be owl by herself.

What did the pig farmer give her husband for Valentine's Day?

Hogs and kisses.

### What kind of flower do you never want to receive on Valentine's Day?

A cauliflower.

### What did the bat say to his friend?

"It's fun hanging out with you."

### What did the drum say to its sweetheart?

"My heart beats for you."

What did one bee say
to the other bee?

"I love bee-ing
with you."

Where do kittens buy presents
for other kittens?

From cat-alogues.

What did the baker
say to his wife?

"I'm do-nuts
about you."

Where do hamburgers go to dance with their friends?

Meat-balls.

Knock Knock!

Who's there?

**Pooch.**

Pooch, who?

**Pooch your arms around me and give me a hug.**

What did one cat say to the other cat?

"You're purrr-fect for me."

## Did you hear about the bed bugs that fell in love?

They're getting married in the spring.

## What happened when the vampires went on a date?

It was love at first bite.

## What did one orca say to the other orca?

"Whale you be mine?"

**Why do squirrels never get married?**

They'd drive each other nuts.

**What do you call two birds in love?**

Tweet-hearts.

**How do animals that live underground send love letters?**

By e-mole.

**Anna:** Do you have a date for Valentine's Day?

Millie: Yes, it's the 14$^{th}$ of February.

**What did one sheep say to the other sheep?**

"Wool you marry me?"

**Boy:** I love u.

Girl: Oh, really?

**Boy:** Yes, it's my favourite letter.

243

Who loves to go to summer parties but is never invited?

Ants.

Did you hear about the shortsighted porcupine?

He fell in love with a pincushion.

Knock Knock!

Who's there?

Frank.

Frank, who?

Frank you for being my friend.

**What flowers did the monkey get for Valentine's Day?**

Forget-me-nuts.

**Big sister: I can marry anyone I please.**

Little brother: But you don't please anyone.

**What did the calculator say to the pencil?**

"You can always count on me."

**Boy:** I can't leave you.

Girl: You love me that much?

**Boy:** It's not that. You're standing on my foot!

**What did the envelope say to the stamp?**

"Stick with me and we'll go places."

**Where is a wall's favourite place to meet its friend?**

At the corner.

Knock Knock!

Who's there?

Keith.

Keith, who?

Keith me, thweetheart!

How do skeletons
call their friends?

On the tele-bone.

How do you propose
over the phone?

Just give them a ring.

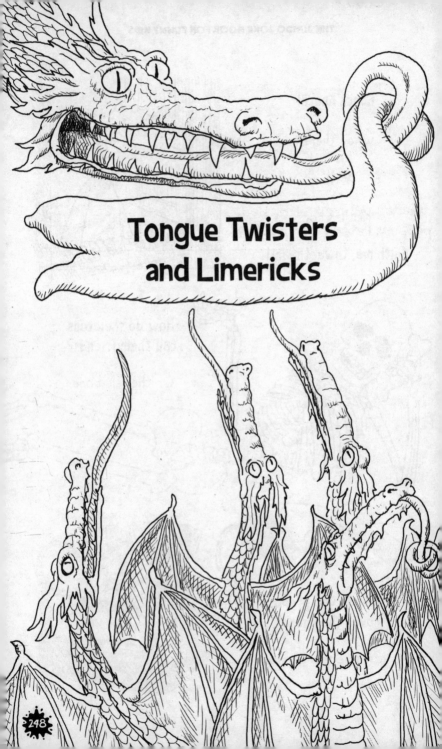

# Tongue Twisters
# and Limericks

Peter Piper picked a
peck of pickled peppers.
A peck of pickled peppers
Peter Piper picked.
If Peter Piper picked a
peck of pickled peppers,
where's the peck of pickled
peppers Peter Piper picked?

There was an old man from Peru,
who dreamed he was
eating his shoe.
He woke in the night,
with a terrible fright,
to find out it was
perfectly true.

If a dog
chews shoes,
which shoes does
it choose?

The big black bug bit
the big black bear,
but the big black bear
bit the big black bug back.

There was a young
man from Bengal,
who went to a
masquerade ball.
He dressed, just for fun,
as a hamburger bun,
and a dog ate him up
in the hall.

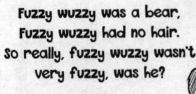

Fuzzy wuzzy was a bear,
Fuzzy wuzzy had no hair.
So really, fuzzy wuzzy wasn't
very fuzzy, was he?

I wish to wash my
Irish wristwatch.

A skunk sat on a stump and thunk the stump stunk,
but the stump thunk the skunk stunk.

How much wood would a woodchuck chuck
if a woodchuck could chuck wood?
He would chuck, he would, as much as he could,
and chuck as much wood, as a woodchuck would
if a woodchuck could chuck wood.

I saw Susie sitting
in a shoe shine shop.
Where she shines, she sits,
and where she sits,
she shines.

The great Greek grape
growers grow great
Greek grapes.

Six thick thistle
sticks are six
sticks thick.

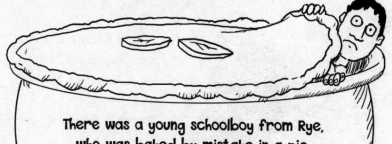

There was a young schoolboy from Rye,
who was baked by mistake in a pie.
To his mother's disgust,
he emerged through the crust,
and exclaimed, with a yawn, "Where am I?"

Leaping lizards like
to lick lovely lemon
lollipops for lunch.

Betty Botter had some butter,
"But," she said, "this butter's bitter.
If I bake this bitter butter,
it would make my batter bitter.
But a bit of better butter –
that would make my batter better."

Give papa a cup of proper coffee in a copper coffee cup.

Kitty caught the kitten in the kitchen.

A pleasant place to place a plaice is a place where a plaice is pleased to be placed.

There once were two
cats from Kilkenny.
Each thought that was
one cat too many,
so they started to fight
and to scratch and to bite.
Now, instead of two cats,
there aren't any.

Whether the weather be fine,
or whether the weather be not,
whether the weather be cold,
or whether the weather be hot,
we'll weather the weather,
whatever the weather,
whether we like it or not.

The sixth sick shepherd's
sixth sheep's sick.

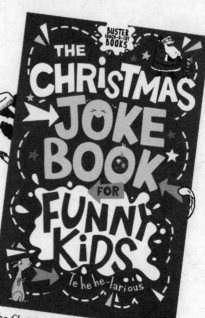

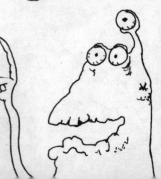